1. **Sir Lawrence Alma-Tadema.** *A Coign of Vantage,* 1895.

Art Masterpieces to Color

60 Great Paintings from Botticelli to Picasso

Rendered by Marty Noble

DOVER PUBLICATIONS, INC.
Mineola, New York

INTRODUCTION

Have you ever wanted to create a memorable work of art? With this unique collection, covering a wide range of styles and movements, now art lovers of all ages can experiment by altering the colors and hues of some very well-known masterpieces of art. Included here are sixty black-and-white line renderings of artistic treasures by some of the greatest artists in history, among them Botticelli, Vermeer, Goya, Degas, van Gogh, and Picasso.

To color these magnificent paintings, aspiring artists may use watercolors, crayons, markers, acrylics, felt-tip pens, or any other type of media. Color renditions of the original works are featured on the covers of this book if you want to reproduce the artist's colors. Just remember that there is no right or wrong way to color these artworks. Explore your own creativity by mixing different styles and artists. Why don't you try Seurat's Pointillist technique on a different painting and see what happens? Or, change the color and tone of El Greco's gloomy *View of Toledo* to see how it affects its interpretation.

These plates are printed on one side only, so dark markers and paints will not show through. While you're working, you may also want to slide a piece of cardboard between the pages so that the colors won't bleed. To remove a page for framing, please carefully cut along the gray dotted line with an X-ACTO knife. The paintings are arranged alphabetically by artist. A section of brief notes about each artist and painting begins on page 121, following the plates.

Copyright

Copyright © 2004 by Dover Publications, Inc.
All rights reserved.

Bibliographical Note

Art Masterpieces to Color: 60 Great Paintings from Botticelli to Picasso
is a new work, first published by Dover Publications, Inc., in 2004.

International Standard Book Number: 0-486-43381-1

Manufactured in the United States of America
Dover Publications, Inc., 31 East 2nd Street, Mineola, N.Y. 11501

2. **Sandro Botticelli.** *The Birth of Venus*, ca. 1485.

3. **William-Adolphe Bouguereau.** *Young Girl Defending Herself against Eros, 1880.*

4. **Pieter Bruegel.** *The Peasant Dance, 1567–68.*

5. **Sir Edward Burne-Jones.** *An Angel Playing a Flageolet, 1878.*

6. **Mary Cassatt.** *Young Mother Sewing,* 1902.

7. **Paul Cézanne.** *The Blue Vase,* 1885–87.

8. **Marc Chagall.** *The Fiddler,* 1912.

9. **William Merritt Chase.** *Portrait of Miss Dora Wheeler,* 1883.

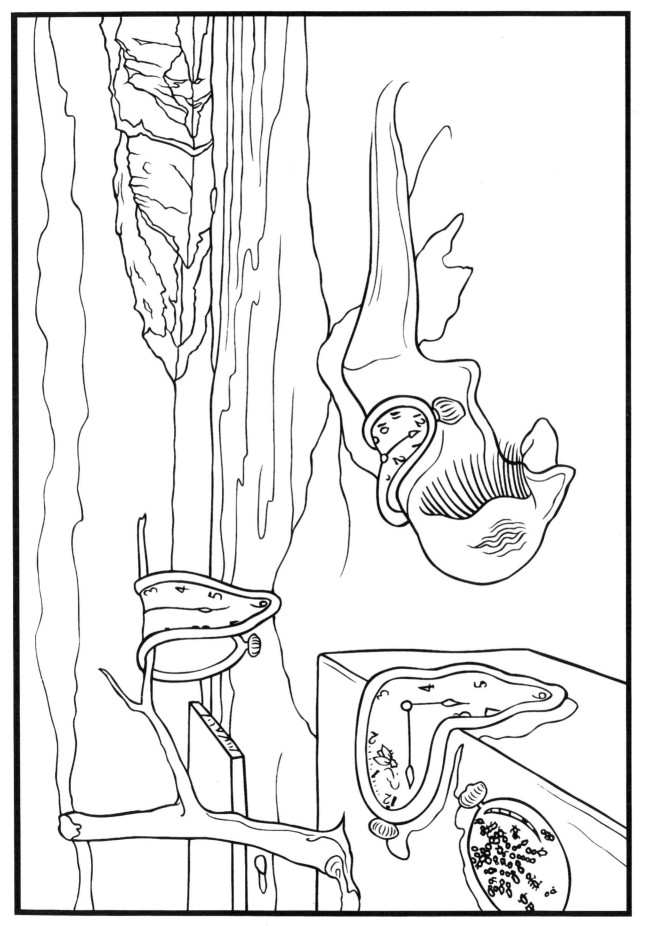

10. **Salvador Dalí.** *The Persistence of Memory,* 1931.

11. **Edgar Degas.** *Before the Exam (The Dancing Class),* 1880.

12. **Albrecht Dürer.** *The Madonna with the Iris,* 1508.

13. **Thomas Eakins.** *The Champion Single Sculls (Max Schmitt in a Single Scull)*, 1871.

14. **Jean Honoré Fragonard.** *A Young Girl Reading,* 1776.

15. **Thomas Gainsborough.** *The Blue Boy,* ca. 1770.

16. **Paul Gauguin.** *When Will You Marry?*, 1892.

17. **William Glackens.** *Chez Mouquin,* 1905.

18. **Vincent van Gogh.** *Van Gogh's Bedroom*, 1888.

19. **Francisco Goya.** *Don Manuel Osorio Manrique de Zuñiga,* 1787.

20. **El Greco.** *View of Toledo*, 1604–14.

21. **Frans Hals.** *The Laughing Cavalier,* 1624.

22. **Edward Hicks.** *The Peaceable Kingdom, ca. 1837.*

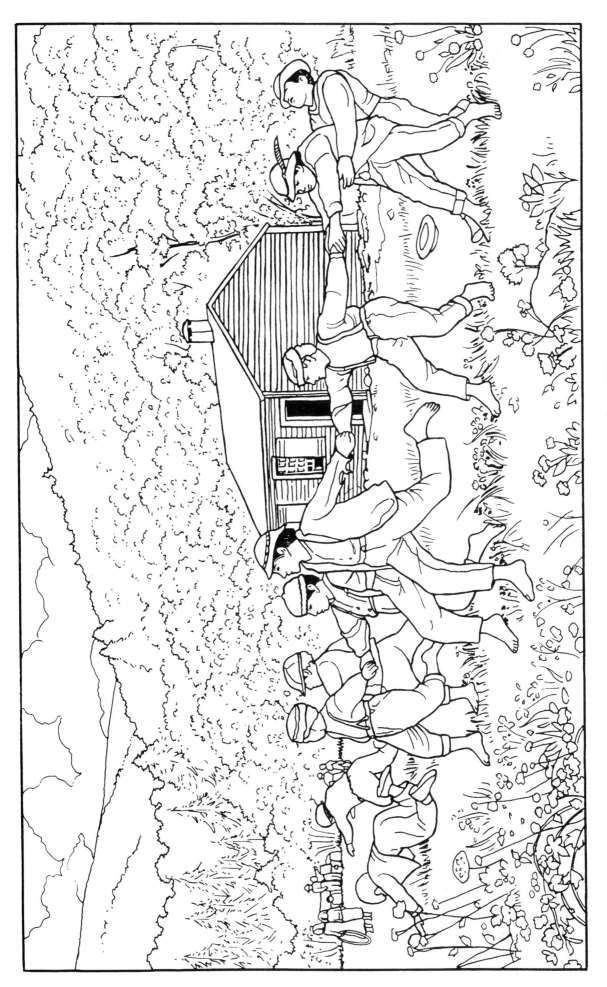

23. **Winslow Homer**. *Snap the Whip.* 1872.

24. **Edward Hopper.** *Hotel Room,* 1931.

25. **Frida Kahlo.** *Self-Portrait with Monkey,* 1940.

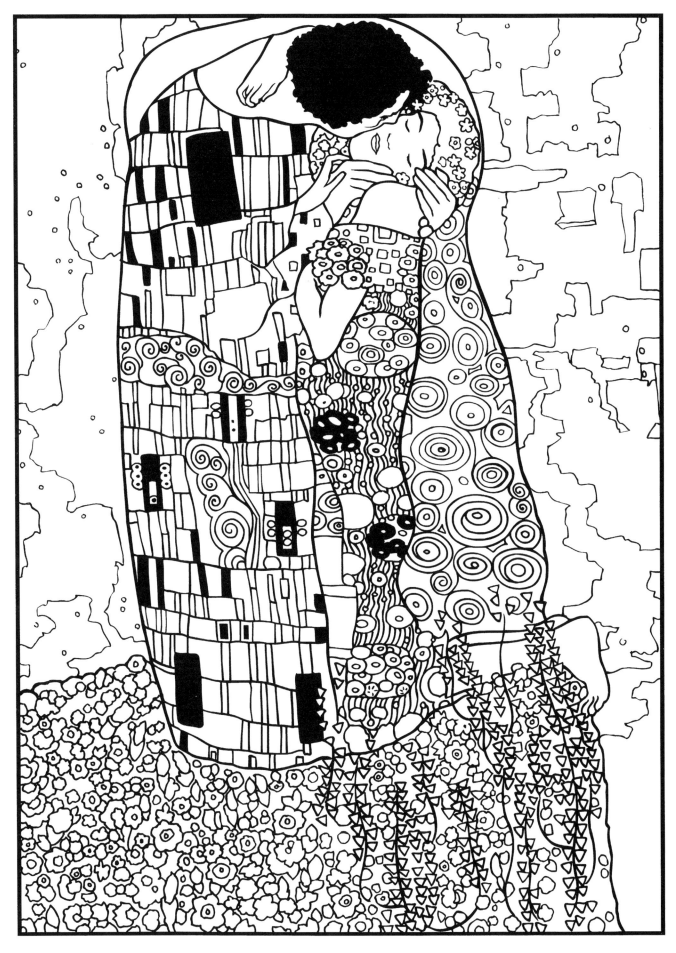

26. **Gustav Klimt.** *The Kiss,* 1907–08.

27. **Frederic, Lord Leighton.** *Flaming June,* 1895.

28. **Leonardo da Vinci.** *Mona Lisa,* 1506.

29. **Emanuel Leutze.** *Washington Crossing the Delaware,* 1851.

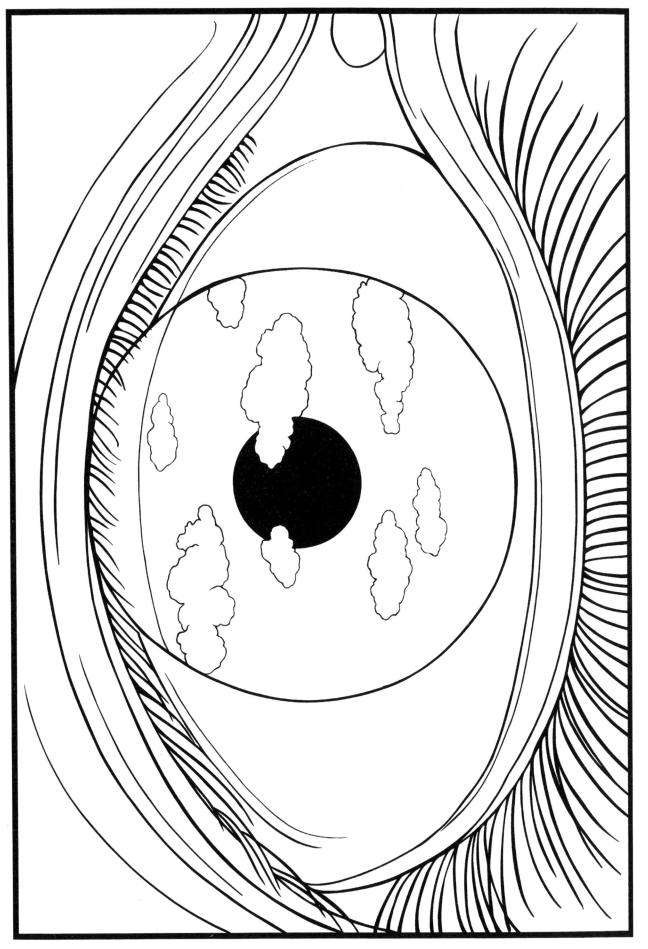

30. **René Magritte.** *The False Mirror,* 1935.

31. Édouard Manet. *A Bar at the Folies-Bergère*, 1881.

32. **Henri Matisse.** *Harmony in Red,* 1908.

33. **Michelangelo Buonarroti.** *Delphic Sibyl,* 1508–12.

34. Jean-François Millet. *The Gleaners*, 1857.

35. **Joan Miró.** *People and Dogs Before the Sun*, 1949.

36. **Amedeo Modigliani.** *Lunia Czechowska with a Fan,* 1919.

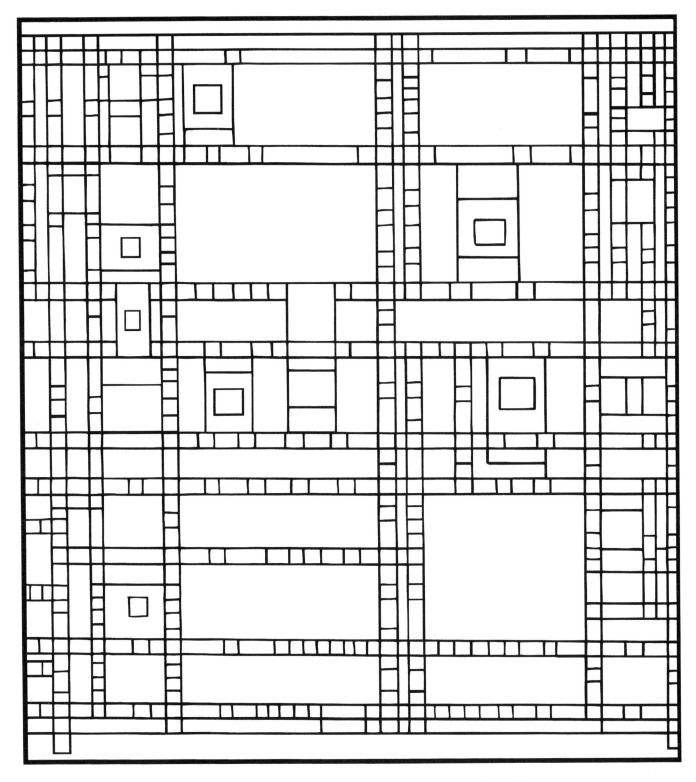

37. **Piet Mondrian.** *Broadway Boogie-Woogie,* 1942–43.

38. **Claude Monet.** *Sunflowers,* 1881.

39. **Grandma Moses.** *A Beautiful World*, 1948.

40. **Edvard Munch.** *The Scream,* 1893.

41. **Bartolomé Murillo.** *The Little Fruit Seller,* 1670–75.

42. **Pablo Picasso.** *Les Demoiselles d'Avignon,* 1907.

43. **Camille Pissarro.** *Chrysanthemums in a Chinese Vase,* 1873.

44. **Raphael.** *The Sistine Madonna,* 1513–14.

45. **Odilon Redon.** *Wildflowers,* 1905.

46. **Rembrandt van Rijn.** *Aristotle Contemplating the Bust of Homer,* 1653.

47. **Pierre-Auguste Renoir.** *Luncheon of the Boating Party,* 1880–81.

48. **Diego Rivera.** *Flower Day,* 1925.

49. **Dante Gabriel Rossetti.** *La Pia de' Tolomei,* 1868–80.

50. **Henri Rousseau.** *The Sleeping Gypsy,* 1897.

51. **Peter Paul Rubens.** *Portrait of Susanne Fourment,* 1625.

52. **John Singer Sargent.** *Paul Helleu Sketching with His Wife, 1889.*

53. **Georges Seurat.** *Sunday Afternoon on the Island of La Grande Jatte, 1884–86.*

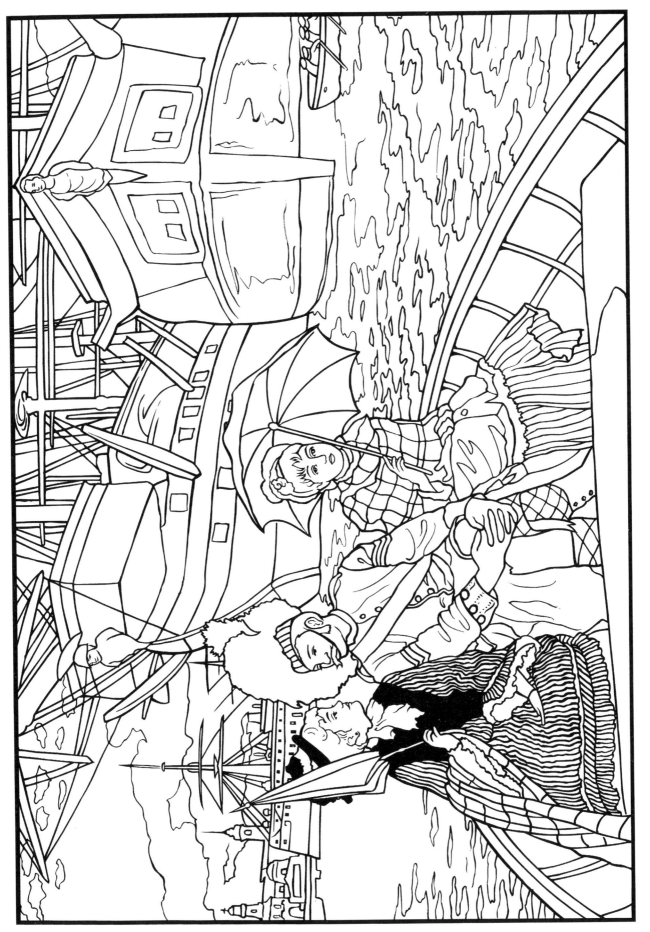

54. **James Tissot**. *Portsmouth Dockyard, 1877.*

55. Henri de Toulouse-Lautrec. *La Goulue Arriving at the Moulin Rouge with Two Women,* 1892.

56. **Diego Velázquez.** *Infanta Margarita,* 1660.

57. **Jan Vermeer.** *Girl with a Pearl Earring,* 1660.

58. **John William Waterhouse.** *A Mermaid,* 1901.

59. **Jean-Antoine Watteau.** *Pierrot: Gilles,* 1721.

60. **Grant Wood.** *American Gothic,* 1930.

1. Sir Lawrence Alma-Tadema (1836–1912). *A Coign of Vantage,* 1895. Oil on canvas, 25¼ in. x 17¾ in. A painter of classical genre scenes, Alma-Tadema was born in the Netherlands and studied at the Antwerp Academy of Art. He specialized in subjects from Greek, Roman, and Egyptian antiquity. Although his paintings usually portrayed a romanticized vision, Alma-Tadema felt that historical accuracy was of prime importance. His meticulously painted pictures were very popular among the Victorian middle classes and he produced over 400 paintings in his lifetime.

2. Sandro Botticelli (ca. 1445–1510). *The Birth of Venus,* ca. 1485. Tempera on canvas, 68 in. x 110 in. Born in Florence, Italy, Botticelli began his artistic training under Filippo Lippi. He painted mostly portraits and religious works. He is best known, however, for his treatment of mythological subjects, notably, *The Birth of Venus.* Perhaps his most adored painting, *The Birth of Venus* depicts Venus rising from a gilded scallop shell. Although he died in obscurity, Botticelli was rediscovered in the nineteenth century by the Pre-Raphaelites, who greatly admired the work of the Renaissance artist.

3. William-Adolphe Bouguereau (1825–1905). *Young Girl Defending Herself against Eros,* 1880. Oil on canvas, 63⁵⁄₁₆ in. x 44⅞ in. With over 700 finished works, Bouguereau enjoyed a long, successful career as an academic painter. His superb paintings of religious, mythological, and genre subjects are carefully composed and painstakingly executed. A staunch supporter of the academic Salon painters, Bouguereau opposed the admission of Impressionist works to the Salon, believing them to be no more than unfinished sketches. In 1895, Bouguereau explained his art philosophy by stating, ". . . there's only one kind of painting. It is the painting that presents the eye with perfection, the kind of beautiful and impeccable enamel you find in Veronese and Titian." Bouguereau's exquisite paintings portray his love of rich color, his remarkable technical proficiency, and his passion for the classics.

4. Pieter Bruegel (ca. 1525–1569). *The Peasant Dance,* 1567–68. Oil on panel, 44⅞ in. x 64½ in. Based on real-life observation, the work of Bruegel often depicted the peasants in his native landscape, earning him the nickname "Peasant Bruegel." Around 1551, he began to travel through France and Italy, later settling in Brussels, where he completed his major works. His lively genre paintings of peasant life reach their finest expression in *The Blind Leading the Blind, The Peasant Wedding,* and *The Peasant Dance.*

5. Sir Edward Burne-Jones (1833–1898). *An Angel Playing a Flageolet,* 1878. Watercolor, 29½ in. x 24 in. Pre-Raphaelite painter Sir Edward Burne-Jones was educated at the University of Oxford and settled in London, where he became a pupil of Dante Gabriel Rossetti. The two artists shared the ideals of the Pre-Raphaelites, a small but influential group of artists who wanted to recapture the simplicity and high moral tone of medieval painting and design. Burne-Jones's paintings, which depict classical, medieval, and biblical themes, are noted for their dreamy, romanticized style and sentimentality.

6. Mary Cassatt (1844–1926). *Young Mother Sewing,* 1902. Oil on canvas, 36¾ in. x 29 in. Born in Pennsylvania, Cassatt was the only American member of the Impressionists. She studied art at the Pennsylvania Academy of Art and then traveled to Europe, spending most of her life in Paris. Professionally, she was greatly influenced by her close friend, French Impressionist painter Edgar Degas. Cassatt painted family scenes of mothers and children, and achieved recognition for these tender representations. She was also very much influenced by Japanese woodcuts, and excelled in making woodcut prints. Her eyesight began to fail in 1900, and Cassatt stopped working by 1914.

7. Paul Cézanne (1839–1906). *The Blue Vase,* 1885–87. Oil on canvas, 24⅜ in. x 20⅛ in. French Postimpressionist painter Paul Cézanne was the only son of a wealthy banker. His early works had a dark, somber tone that brightened after he began to paint outdoors with Pissarro in 1872. Dissatisfied with the Impressionists' sole reliance on light effects, Cézanne concentrated on the use of geometric form and construction. A prime influence on twentieth-century art, notably Cubism, Cézanne created effects of depth and solidity by varying the interaction of planes of paint, parallel brushstroke, and intense color. His compositions include portraits of himself and his family, over 200 still lifes, and many variations of L'Estaque and Mont Sainte-Victoire landscapes.

8. Marc Chagall (1887–1985). *The Fiddler,* 1912. Oil on canvas, 74 in. x 62¼ in. Russian-born painter and designer Marc Chagall developed a highly individual and personalized style, incorporating elements of Russian Expressionism, Surrealism, and Cubism. A unique blend of reality and dreams, his art is suffused with poetic imagery and striking visual metaphors. Most of his subject matter is rooted in the Russian-Jewish folklore of his childhood. His recurring motifs, such as rooftop fiddlers and floating brides, possess a surrealistic quality and frequently appear in a dreamlike setting. In his work, richly colored figures predominate within a loosely related series of images, providing a visual montage of Chagall's own life experiences. He also designed stained glass windows, mosaics, and theater sets.

9. William Merritt Chase (1849–1916). *Portrait of Miss Dora Wheeler,* 1883. Oil on canvas, 62½ in. x 65¼ in. Admired for his portraits, landscapes, and everyday scenes, Chase was born in Indiana and studied in Munich. He returned to the U.S. and gained a fine reputation as a teacher. Dora Wheeler, the subject of this portrait, was Chase's first pupil upon his return from Europe. Chase was particularly influenced by James McNeill Whistler, and even adopted that artist's flat, decorative style for a time.

10. Salvador Dalí (1904–1989). *The Persistence of Memory,* 1931. Oil on canvas, 9½ in. x 13 in. Spanish painter Salvador Dalí studied at the Academy of Fine Arts in Madrid before moving to Paris. As a member of the Surrealist movement, Dalí promoted the idea of absurdity and the role of the unconscious in his art. Influenced by the psychoanalytic theories of Freud and abnormal psychology in general, he developed a range of unforgettable imagery, including distortions of the human form and limp watches, as seen in *The*

Persistence of Memory, Dalí's most well-known painting. He also painted religious themes as well as numerous portraits of his wife.

11. Edgar Degas (1834–1917). *Before the Exam (The Dancing Class),* 1880. Pastel on paper, 24¾ in. x 18½ in. Born in Paris, France, Degas taught himself to paint by copying the Old Masters in the Louvre. He enrolled at the École des Beaux Arts and began to take an interest in painting modern life subjects. Degas painted the subtle movements of musicians, ballet dancers, and other stage performers in elegant, painstaking detail. These kinds of subjects afforded him the opportunity to depict fleeting moments in time and unusual angles. Akin to the view through the lens of a camera, Degas's paintings are infused with novel, unique perspectives that have come to epitomize his work.

12. Albrecht Dürer (1471–1528). *The Madonna with the Iris,* 1508. Oil on lime, 58¾ in. x 46⅛ in. The leading figure of the Northern European Renaissance, German painter and engraver Albrecht Dürer was born in Nuremburg and traveled widely in Europe. An accomplished painter of altarpieces and self-portraits, he was renowned—even in his own day—for his graphic works. Dürer was highly skilled in drawing, and his prints are exemplary for their detail and precision. His innovative prints, ranging in theme from exotic animals to religious and mythological scenes, were admired and copied by other artists across Europe. Dürer perfected the technique of woodcut illustrations, producing series such as the *Apocalypse* (1498).

13. Thomas Eakins (1844–1916). *The Champion Single Sculls (Max Schmitt in a Single Scull),* 1871. Oil on canvas, 32¼ in. x 46¼ in. Born in Philadelphia, Eakins attended anatomy classes in America and studied art in Paris and Spain, where he was dazzled by Diego Velázquez's naturalism. In the early 1870s, Eakins began to paint rowing pictures. This work, among his most famous, depicts his boyhood friend Max Schmitt, a champion oarsman. In the distance, the artist himself rows away from the viewer in a boat. Celebrated for his realistic depiction of the contemporary world, Eakins exerted a considerable influence through his teaching.

14. Jean Honoré Fragonard (1732–1806). *A Young Girl Reading,* 1776. Oil on canvas, 32 in. x 26 in. Fragonard, a gifted painter in the Rococo style, had studied under Chardin and Boucher, who encouraged him to compete for the Prix de Rome, which he won in 1752. He then went to the French Academy in Rome in 1756, remaining there until 1761. A master technician and brilliant colorist, Fragonard painted genre pictures of contemporary life and landscapes that foreshadowed Impressionism. His reputation rests on his amorous scenes, rustic landscapes, and decorative panels. Able to convey joyful human emotion on his canvases, Fragonard completed about 500 paintings, 1,000 drawings, and numerous illustrations and etchings.

15. Thomas Gainsborough (1727–1788). *The Blue Boy,* ca. 1770. Oil on canvas, 70 in. x 48 in. Considered one of the great masters of portraiture and landscape, English painter Thomas Gainsborough developed an elegant style of painting and became a founding member of the Royal Academy. In 1774 he accepted a royal invitation to paint portraits of King George III and his family and soon became wealthy through numerous commissions from society's elite. In his lifetime, Gainsborough executed more than 500 paintings—over 200 of them portraits. His portraits are characterized by graceful figures and thinly applied brushstrokes in delicate, cool colors. *The Blue Boy* is a portrait of Jonathan Buttall, the son of one of the artist's friends.

16. Paul Gauguin (1848–1903). *When Will You Marry?,* 1892. Oil on canvas, 40 in. x 30½ in. A major precursor of modern art, French artist Paul Gauguin pioneered an appreciation of the simple and primitive in art. Generally regarded as one of the greatest of the Postimpressionists, he depicted peasant life in Brittany early in his career and spent the last ten years of his life painting in Tahiti and the Marquesas Islands. His Breton style, characterized by flat contoured figures, gradually matured into the richly colored works of his later South Seas period. His Tahitian works—among his most famous—are comprised of native figures and landscapes with strong outlines and flat, bold colors.

17. William Glackens (1870–1938). *Chez Mouquin,* 1905. Oil on canvas, 48 in. x 39 in. Born in Philadelphia, William Glackens studied at the Pennsylvania Academy of Fine Arts under the instruction of painter Robert Henri. Glackens was a member of the Ashcan school and was also one of "The Eight," a group of realist painters who exhibited their works together in 1908. Strongly influenced by the Impressionists, he painted subjects from everyday urban life as well as scenes of fashionable society.

18. Vincent van Gogh (1853–1890). *Van Gogh's Bedroom,* 1888. Oil on canvas, 28¾ in. x 36¼ in. The Dutch Postimpressionist painter tried such varied careers as language teacher, art dealer, and preacher before he began to paint in earnest in 1880. Expressive brushwork, the heightened use of color, and an intense emotionality typify van Gogh's unique style. His attempt to organize an artists' community in Arles with Toulouse-Lautrec and Gauguin proved to be unsuccessful. Van Gogh's volatile career lasted merely one decade; he took his own life in 1890. Although he sold just one painting during his lifetime, van Gogh produced 800 oil paintings and 700 drawings.

19. Francisco Goya (1746–1828). *Don Manuel Osorio Manrique de Zuñiga,* 1787. Oil on canvas, 50 in. x 40 in. After Goya was appointed painter to the King of Spain in 1786, the conde de Altamira asked him to paint his son's portrait. The child holds a magpie on a string, while three cats stare wide-eyed at the bird, traditionally a Christian symbol of the soul. In Baroque art, birds symbolized innocence. Goya may have intended this portrait to be a commentary on the fleeting nature of youthful innocence. At the time of his death, Goya had completed over 500 oil paintings and nearly 300 etchings and lithographs.

20. El Greco (ca. 1541–1614). *View of Toledo,* 1604–14. Oil on canvas, 47½ in. x 43 in. El Greco was born in Crete and studied in Italy, most likely a pupil of Titian. Around 1577, he settled in Toledo, Spain, where he established himself as a leading painter. He painted elegant portraits and intensely emotional religious scenes. As El Greco's only true landscape, *View of Toledo* is an expressive rendering of the city, a subject that he frequently used in the background of his works. The sharp white light evokes both the eerie beauty of the place and the menace inherent in nature.

21. Frans Hals (ca. 1580–1666). *The Laughing Cavalier,* 1624. Oil on canvas, 33¾ in. x 27⅛ in. Flemish-born painter Frans Hals was a prolific portraitist who provided his sitters with a good likeness at a reasonable price. His lively portraits are characterized by rapid brushwork that captured fleeting expressions. The suave gentleman depicted in *The Laughing Cavalier,* although unknown, was a young man of twenty-six at the time of the painting. His facial features, including his jaunty moustache and goatee, are precisely detailed, as is his layered collar, which is a masterpiece of brushwork. Hals's work greatly impressed such nineteenth-century artists as Manet and Sargent.

22. Edward Hicks (1780–1849). *The Peaceable Kingdom,* ca. 1837. Oil on canvas, 29 in. x 36 in. A Quaker preacher in Bucks County, Pennsylvania, Edward Hicks supported his large family through the income derived from his painting. It is presumed that Hicks painted over one hundred different versions of *The Peaceable Kingdom* between 1820 and his death. The theme is drawn from Chapter 11 of the Book of Isaiah in the Bible, interpreted by Christianity as a prophecy of the coming of Christ and the arrival of a peaceful world. In many versions, such as the one depicted here, Hicks incorporates a secular vignette of fellow Quaker William Penn's treaty with the Native Americans, which had brought about a measure of a "peaceable kingdom" on earth.

23. Winslow Homer (1836–1910). *Snap the Whip,* 1872. Oil on canvas, 22¼ in. x 36½ in. Painted in an era when art was often steeped in sentimentality, the works of Winslow Homer stand out as refreshing examples of frank realism. One of America's indisputable masters, he produced a series of distinctive images of the sea that is unparalleled in American art. In *Snap the Whip,* Homer, clearly influenced by the French *plein air* technique, depicts boys at play in a country landscape.

24. Edward Hopper (1882–1967). *Hotel Room,* 1931. Oil on canvas, 60 in. x 65 in. Twentieth-century Realist painter Edward Hopper is best known for his paintings that seem to emphasize the loneliness and alienation found in our society. Born in Nyack, New York, Hopper studied commercial art before switching his efforts to fine art. He studied with Robert Henri, a member of the Ashcan school of painters, who typically painted scenes of city life. Hopper traveled to Europe three times between 1906 and 1910, but he remained unaffected by the avant-garde art movements burgeoning there. Taken as a whole, Hopper's work poignantly evokes the essence of American urban life.

25. Frida Kahlo (1907–1954). *Self-Portrait with Monkey,* 1940. Oil on masonite, 21¾ in. x 17⅛ in. Surrealist painter Frida Kahlo was the daughter of a Hungarian Jew and a Mexican Indian. She had polio as a child and attended a university in her hometown of Mexico City. When she was eighteen, Kahlo learned how to paint while recuperating from a crippling bus accident. In 1929, she married Mexican muralist Diego Rivera, who painted politically themed murals commissioned for public buildings. A supporter of Communism, Kahlo often used themes from Mexican folk art in her paintings. A large number of her paintings, like the one seen here, were self-portraits with meaningful symbols.

26. Gustav Klimt (1862–1918). *The Kiss,* 1907–08. Oil on canvas, 70⅞ in. x 70⅞ in. Austrian painter Gustav Klimt revolted against academic art in favor of a decorative style similar to Art Nouveau. In one of his most famous works, *The Kiss,* a mass of patterns and shapes dominates his representation of a kissing couple. Klimt was primarily a decorator, but he did produce murals and a number of portraits as well as allegorical and mythical paintings. His work had a profound impact on Oskar Kokoschka and Egon Schiele.

27. Frederic, Lord Leighton (1830–1896). *Flaming June,* 1895. Oil on canvas, 48 in. x 48 in. English painter and sculptor Frederic Leighton was trained in Europe and lived in Paris from 1855 to 1859, where he met Ingres, Delacroix, Corot, and Millet. Of the highest in quality, his Victorian-era works usually depicted historical, biblical, and classical themes. He moved to London in 1860 and was closely associated with the Pre-Raphaelites. Of all his paintings, *Flaming June* is Leighton's most recognizable and best-loved work. His genius as a colorist and a Classicist are clearly evident in this sensuous painting of a sleeping woman.

28. Leonardo da Vinci (1452–1519). *Mona Lisa,* 1506. Oil on panel, 30¼ in. x 20¾ in. Famous all over the world for her enigmatic smile, the *Mona Lisa* is one of the few paintings by the most esteemed of the Italian Renaissance masters, Leonardo da Vinci. This great work employs an oil painting technique known as *sfumato* that Leonardo specially created to allow himself to use subtle shading. Equally accomplished in anatomy, engineering, and scientific pursuits, Leonardo completed a surprisingly small number of paintings during his lifetime. His diverse talents are showcased in his numerous drawings and sketchbooks.

29. Emanuel Leutze (1816–1868). *Washington Crossing the Delaware,* 1851. Oil on canvas, 149 in. x 255 in. Among the most popular historical painters in America in the mid-nineteenth century, Emanuel Leutze was born in Germany but was reared in Philadelphia. His most famous work was *Washington Crossing the Delaware,* the first version of which was destroyed in a bombing raid during World War II. This version of the work, enormously popular in both America and Germany, was placed on exhibition in New York in 1851. Many studies for the painting still exist, as well as the engraving that was published in 1853 and circulated widely.

30. René Magritte (1898–1967). *The False Mirror,* 1935. Oil on canvas, 7½ in. x 10½ in. Born in Belgium, Magritte began his career as a wallpaper designer and commercial artist. His Surrealist paintings often use fantastic, dreamlike images. Acclaimed as an early innovator of the Pop Art movement of the 1960s, his paintings often focused on visual paradoxes and incongruous images taken out of context. Using symbols including mirrors, eyes, windows, stages, curtains, and pictures within pictures, Magritte demonstrated the illusions of visual perception.

31. Édouard Manet (1832–1883). *A Bar at the Folies-Bergère,* 1881. Oil on canvas, 37½ in. x 51 in. French painter and printmaker Édouard Manet was the son of a high-ranking government official who denounced Manet's inclination toward art. Although Manet's art was strongly rooted in the classics, he was often criticized for his modernity. The Salon rejected several of his paintings due to their controversial subjects. Having adopted the style of painting out-of-doors, Manet was a greatly respected practitioner of Impressionism, though he did not participate in the official exhibitions of the group. Manet's last major painting, *A Bar at the Folies-Bergère,* is one of his most compelling pieces.

32. Henri Matisse (1869–1954). *Harmony in Red,* 1908. Oil on canvas, 71 in. x 97 in. French artist Henri Matisse abandoned his early studies in law to attend the Académie Julian and the École des Beaux Arts in Paris when he was in his early twenties. Matisse, the most famous representative of the art movement known as Fauvism, used bold color to stir the emotions of viewers. The Fauvists ("wild beasts") created innovative works of vivid intensity through their use of pure color. Matisse's later works included more abstraction, as in his collages of colored paper cutouts.

33. Michelangelo Buonarroti (1475–1564). *Delphic Sibyl,* 1508–12. Fresco, 137¾ in. x 149½ in. Italian painter and sculptor Michelangelo spent three years studying with Florentine painter Domenico Ghirlandaio. His extraordinary talents dominated the High Renaissance period. The marble *David,* his most revered work, set the definitive standard in nude sculpture. In 1505, he was commissioned by Pope Julius II to repaint the ceiling of the Sistine Chapel in the Vatican. He illustrated nine biblical scenes extracted from the Book of Genesis as well as images from classical mythology. Depicted here is the figure of the Delphic Sibyl that appears on the frescoed ceiling of the Sistine Chapel.

34. Jean-François Millet (1814–1875). *The Gleaners,* 1857. Oil on canvas, 33 in. x 43 in. French genre and landscape artist Jean-François Millet farmed with his peasant father before focusing his efforts on painting. He achieved recognition in the Salon of 1844 and later settled in Barbizon, where he painted the rustic life of France with sensitivity. In *The Gleaners,* Millet sympathetically depicts three peasant women, who withstand their backbreaking labor with silent dignity. Millet also produced charcoal drawings of high quality.

35. Joan Miró (1893–1983). *People and Dogs Before the Sun,* 1949. Tempera on canvas, 31¾ in. x 21½ in. Born in Barcelona, Joan Miró manifested an inclination toward art early in life. He studied at the La Lonja School of Fine Arts, where one of his instructors called his attention to Catalan primitive art—an influence that continued throughout the artist's career. Although his early works reflect the influences of Cézanne, van Gogh, Cubism and Fauvism, Miró soon allied himself firmly with the Surrealist movement. His work underwent a long and complex development, but some common elements include the bold use of color and curvilinear shapes. He also produced collages, ceramics, murals, etchings, and lithographs.

36. Amedeo Modigliani (1884–1920). *Lunia Czechowska with a Fan,* 1919. Oil on canvas, 39¼ in. x 25½ in. After studying art in Florence and Venice, Modigliani came to Paris, where he struggled with illness, alcohol, and drug addiction. Undoubtedly influenced by Picasso and Cubism, Modigliani also worked briefly in sculpture. He drew directly on his admiration for African sculpture in creating his geometric forms. Modigliani's work consists mainly of painted nudes and richly colored, elongated portraits. He produced

an impressive body of work before dying of tuberculosis at the age of thirty-five.

37. Piet Mondrian (1872–1944). *Broadway Boogie-Woogie,* 1942–43. Oil on canvas, 50 in. x 50 in. A pioneer of abstract art, Dutch painter Piet Mondrian came from an artistic family. After moving to Paris in 1909, his work was greatly influenced by Cubism, and Mondrian's compositions became increasingly more abstract. His first abstract paintings were composed of rhythmical horizontals and verticals, followed by those with geometrical grid patterns. After 1920, he began to paint pictures of colored rectangles with black outlines, a trend that enabled him to focus on the beauty of the simple relationships between pure colors. In *Broadway Boogie-Woogie,* tiny blocks of brilliant color create a pulsing rhythm that jumps from one intersection to another, mimicking the vitality of a New York City street.

38. Claude Monet (1840–1926). *Sunflowers,* 1881. Oil on canvas, 39¾ in. x 32 in. Leading French Impressionist Claude Monet was introduced to the *plein air* style of painting in the 1860s by Boudin. Monet sought to record the "impression" that the subject gave the viewer at that precise time of day, effectively capturing the transient effects of light. Beginning in 1890, he embarked on a series of works that studied the same subject under different light conditions. These works include *Haystacks* and *Water Lilies,* both of which express the subtle nuances of color, light, and atmosphere. Using a bouquet cut from his own garden, Monet's *Sunflowers* differs from his earlier, more realistic reproductions of flowers. The free, unrestrained arrangement foreshadows the later works of van Gogh.

39. Grandma Moses (1860–1961). *A Beautiful World,* 1948. Oil on canvas, 20 in. x 24 in. One of the greatest folk painters of the twentieth century, Grandma Moses first began to paint at the age of seventy-eight. Born on a farm in Greenwich, New York, just before the Civil War, she painted landscape scenes of country life. In 1939, her paintings were exhibited at the Museum of Modern Art in New York City. She produced 2,000 detailed paintings in all, some of which were used on Christmas cards and reproduced in prints. Grandma Moses died at the age of one hundred and one.

40. Edvard Munch (1863–1944). *The Scream,* 1893. Oil on board, 35⅞ in. x 29 in. A forerunner of the Expressionists, Norwegian artist Edvard Munch studied at the Oslo Academy, and then traveled to Paris, where he was largely influenced by the Symbolists and Gauguin. As with many artists, a lot of Munch's subject matter was drawn directly from his own life experiences. He produced intensely powerful images that often portrayed fear, anxiety, love, and death. His iconic painting *The Scream*—one of the best-known images in the history of art—embodies the stress and angst of modern life.

41. Bartolomé Murillo (ca. 1617–1682). *The Little Fruit Seller,* 1670–75. Oil on canvas, 58½ in. x 44½ in. Murillo was born in Seville, Spain, and apprenticed to a local artist. In 1645 he was commissioned to paint a series of eleven paintings depicting scenes from the lives of Franciscan saints. These works brought Murillo fame and earned him a fine reputation. In 1660 Murillo founded the Academy of Fine Arts, a prestigious painting academy in Seville. Although most of his paintings are of a religious nature, Murillo also painted sentimental scenes of children as well as precise portraits. He became the first Spanish painter to achieve widespread European fame.

42. Pablo Picasso (1881–1973). *Les Demoiselles d'Avignon,* 1907. Oil on canvas, 96 in. x 92 in. Spanish artist Pablo Picasso was one of the most inventive painters of the twentieth century. Through his extraordinary imagination and prolific output, Picasso contributed greatly to many disparate styles and major artistic movements. A pivotal work in the development of modern art, *Les Demoiselles d'Avignon* marked a radical break from traditional composition and perspective. In this painting, which paved the way for Cubism, Picasso depicted five nude women in a brothel using flat, angular planes instead of rounded shapes. Although he is most famous for his canvases, he also produced outstanding sculpture, ceramics, graphics, and book illustrations.

43. Camille Pissarro (1830–1903). *Chrysanthemums in a Chinese Vase,* 1873. Oil on canvas, 23¾ in. x 19½ in. One of the founders of Impressionism, Pissarro studied art in Paris, where he was first attracted to the works of the Barbizon school and the realism of Corot. In the 1860s and 1870s, Pissarro lightened his palette and applied brushstrokes of bright color on his canvases to create luminous effects. Along with fellow Impressionist painters Monet, Renoir, and Manet, Pissarro helped organize the first independent Impressionist exhibition in 1874. He also experimented with various artistic styles, such as Pointillism, a technique popularized by Seurat.

44. Raphael (1483–1520). *The Sistine Madonna,* 1513–14. Oil on canvas, 106 in. x 79 in. Studying under Perugino, Raphael established his mastery at seventeen and began receiving high-level commissions. In 1504 he traveled to Florence, where he was strongly influenced by Leonardo and Michelangelo. After completing several of his famous Madonnas, he was summoned to Rome in 1508 to decorate papal chambers in the Vatican. These frescoes in the Stanza della Segnatura are among his greatest work. *The Sistine Madonna* shows the serenity, rich color, and bold composition that is characteristic of his work.

45. Odilon Redon (1840–1916). *Wildflowers,* 1905. Pastel on brown paper, 24⅞ in. x 19¹¹⁄₁₆ in. The greatest of the French Symbolists, Odilon Redon worked almost exclusively in charcoal until his fifties. During the 1890s, he took up painting in pastels and color. After a religious crisis in the early 1890s and a serious illness in 1894–95, the previously unhappy Redon was transformed into a more cheerful personality and expressed himself using radiant colors in mythological scenes and flower paintings. His flower pieces in particular were very much admired by Matisse, and the Surrealists regarded Redon as one of their precursors.

46. Rembrandt van Rijn (1606–1669). *Aristotle Contemplating the Bust of Homer,* 1653. Oil on canvas, 56½ in. x 53¾ in. Dutch painter and etcher Rembrandt was one of the most beloved artists in Europe in the seventeenth century. While his portraits and self-portraits are widely acknowledged as his finest achievements, he also painted religious subjects and produced 300 etchings and over 1,000 drawings. In the painting seen here, completed for a Sicilian nobleman, the Greek philosopher Aristotle rests his hand reflectively on a bust of the epic poet Homer. Aristotle wears a gold chain with a medallion bearing the image of Alexander the Great. The study of a figure lost in thought is characteristic of Rembrandt's work.

47. Pierre-Auguste Renoir (1841–1919). *Luncheon of the Boating Party,* 1880–81. Oil on canvas, 51¼ in. x 68⅛ in. Born in France, Renoir began his art career with an apprenticeship at a factory, where he painted flowers onto porcelain dishes. Along with fellow Impressionist painters Sisley, Bazille, and Monet, Renoir painted landscapes directly from nature to study the effects of light. Using feathery brushstrokes and sparkling bursts of color, Renoir painted over 2,000 portraits in his lifetime. Among his favorite subjects were portraits of women, children, and social scenes of everyday life, as pictured in *Luncheon of the Boating Party.*

48. Diego Rivera (1886–1957). *Flower Day,* 1925. Encaustic on canvas, 58 in. x 47½ in. Mexican painter Diego Rivera received many commissions to paint murals on public buildings. These murals often depicted the life and history of the Mexican people. Married to Surrealist painter Frida Kahlo, Rivera infused his work with a blend of folk art and revolutionary propaganda. *Flower Day,* one of Rivera's signature masterpieces, won a purchase prize in 1925 at an exhibition in Los Angeles. While some critics believe the painting honors an ancient Mexican tradition of dedicating flowers to a god of festivals, others believe that it represents a political statement. In this view, the flower vendor is a symbol of the Mexican middle class, who must shoulder the burden of their whole country.

49. Dante Gabriel Rossetti (1828–1882). *La Pia de' Tolomei,* 1868–80. Oil on canvas, 41¼ in. x 47½ in. Considered the central figure of the Pre-Raphaelite movement, Rossetti was educated at King's College and trained at the Royal Academy schools, but left there in disgust over their dry, classical style. In 1848, he helped to form the Pre-Raphaelite Brotherhood, which aimed to return to pre-Renaissance art forms. He shared his studio with other artists, wrote poetry, and published translations from works of Dante Alighieri and other Italian writers. After the Pre-Raphaelites disbanded, Rossetti worked mainly in watercolor, but returned to oil painting during the 1860s.

50. Henri Rousseau (1844–1910). *The Sleeping Gypsy,* 1897. Oil on canvas, 51 in. x 79 in. A customs officer who painted in his spare time, the French-born Rousseau had no formal artistic training and only devoted himself exclusively to painting after his early retirement at the age of forty. Renowned for his highly stylized works, Rousseau created detailed paintings of lush foliage and mysterious figures in exotic imaginary landscapes. His portraits, still lifes, and junglescapes are initial examples of a manner of painting known as "naïve," a term indicative of the way an artist treated a subject in his or her own visionary way.

51. Peter Paul Rubens (1577–1640). *Portrait of Susanne Fourment,* 1625. Oil on panel, 31¹⁄₁₆ in. x 21¼ in. Flemish painter and diplomat Peter Paul Rubens held apprenticeships in Antwerp before his admission to the painters' guild in 1598. In 1600 he went to Italy, where he performed diplomatic missions for the duke of Mantua. An inventive and prolific artist, he was appointed court painter to the Spanish Hapsburg regents and produced many altarpieces over the next decade. Rubens was the greatest exponent of Baroque painting's sensual exuberance and his profound influence has endured for centuries. This painting is a portrait of the artist's sister-in-law.

52. John Singer Sargent (1856–1925). *Paul Helleu Sketching with His Wife*, 1889. Oil on canvas, 26⅛ in. x 32⅛ in. Portrait painter John Singer Sargent was born in Florence, Italy, to American parents. As a youngster, Sargent traveled with his parents around Europe, and gained experiences that would contribute greatly to his self-assurance with all kinds of people and places. Exquisite portrayals of affluent figures of the day and their families made Sargent a much sought-after artist, and many patrons clamored for his refined, flattering style. Sargent went through a brief Impressionist phase, inspired by the work of Claude Monet at Giverny. In this painting, Sargent employs the French *plein air* technique, depicting Paul Helleu and his wife in natural light when they visited him in the countryside.

53. Georges Seurat (1859–1891). *Sunday Afternoon on the Island of La Grande Jatte*, 1884–86. Oil on canvas, 81 in. x 120 in. Using newly discovered color theories, Post-impressionist painter Georges Seurat painted his subject by placing tiny, precise brushstrokes of color close to one another so that the viewer's eye blends them at a distance. This technique is known as *Pointillism*. The artist drew many different versions of this painting, and completed more than thirty oil sketches to prepare for the final work. His painstaking method is often contrasted with the spontaneity of the Impressionists.

54. James Tissot (1836–1902). *Portsmouth Dockyard*, 1877. Oil on canvas, 15 in. x 21½ in. Known for his charming illustrations of Victorian life, James Tissot was also a caricaturist for *Vanity Fair*, a fashionable portrait painter, and, after 1886, a painter of religious subjects. The French artist settled in London in the 1870s and helped to popularize a new kind of genre painting—scenes of modern life. Unlike some artists, whose talents were only appreciated after their death, Tissot's pictures were loved and purchased by his contemporaries at very high prices. In *Portsmouth Dockyard*, Tissot shows a flirtatious scene where Victorian propriety clashes with a budding social transgression.

55. Henri de Toulouse-Lautrec (1864–1901). *La Goulue Arriving at the Moulin Rouge with Two Women*, 1892. Oil on cardboard, 31¼ in. x 23¼ in. French painter and graphic artist Toulouse-Lautrec began to paint while recuperating from crippling injuries to his legs. In 1884 he established a studio in the Montmartre district of Paris, beginning a life-long association with the area's cafés, cabarets, and entertainers. Noted for his satiric sketches and studies of Parisian nightlife, he exerted a tremendous influence on future artists. Toulouse-Lautrec stands as an innovator, known for his posters and lithographs of individuals from the "seedier" side of life. By simplifying outlines and juxtaposing intense colors, he effortlessly conveys the impression of movement in his subjects.

56. Diego Velázquez (1599–1660). *Infanta Margarita*, 1660. Oil on canvas, 47½ in. x 42⅛ in. Born in Seville, Spain, Velázquez set up his own studio in 1618. His early works were typically domestic genre pieces. After moving to Madrid in 1623, Velázquez took a trip to Italy to study art, and Titian's influence is evident in his color use. Soon after, he was hired as a court painter to Philip IV in Madrid, where he produced outstanding portraits of the royal family as well as religious paintings and genre scenes. He would spend the rest of his life in service of the royal court, in different ranks, eventually becoming curator of the court.

57. Jan Vermeer (1632–1675). *Girl with a Pearl Earring*, 1660. Oil on canvas, 17¾ in. x 15¾ in. Dutch painter Vermeer served as head of the Delft artists' guild twice and worked as an art dealer to support his family. He painted mainly interior genre scenes that depicted aristocratic society. Vermeer's paintings were few in number, and his work was not widely appreciated in his lifetime. *Girl with a Pearl Earring*, universally acknowledged as one of Vermeer's absolute masterworks, possesses a softness that is almost impressionistic in style.

58. John William Waterhouse (1849–1917). *A Mermaid*, 1901. Oil on canvas, 38½ in. x 26¼ in. Painter of classical, historical, and literary subjects, John William Waterhouse was born in Rome to British parents. He attended the Royal Academy in London and traveled on several occasions to Italy, where he painted genre scenes. Though he is often associated with the Pre-Raphaelites, Waterhouse never formally aligned himself with any school of painting. Waterhouse's painting, *A Mermaid*, was exhibited at the Royal Academy in 1901 and portrays a single figure of a mermaid pensively combing her hair.

59. Jean-Antoine Watteau (1684–1721). *Pierrot: Gilles*, 1721. Oil on canvas, 73 in. x 59 in. French Rococo painter Jean-Antoine Watteau was instrumental in developing a new kind of genre painting known as *fêtes galantes* (scenes of gallantry) that depicted an aristocratic pastoral fantasy world. Watteau first went to Paris in 1702 as an apprentice to a painter and was eventually accepted by the French Academy in 1712. In frail health from tuberculosis, Watteau died at an early age. Along with elegant party scenes, much of Watteau's art centers on the themes of music, the theater, and mythical pieces.

60. Grant Wood (1892–1942). *American Gothic*, 1930. Oil on beaverboard, 29 in. x 24½ in. Born in Iowa, Grant Wood asked his dentist and his sister to pose as a farmer and his unmarried daughter for what has become one of the most famous (and most parodied) paintings in the history of American art, *American Gothic*. Although Wood was accused of ridiculing the narrow-mindedness of rural life, he denied the allegation, insisting that his painting was not a caricature of rural America, but a celebration of the values of the Midwest. The painting's title is derived from the Gothic Revival style of the cottage in the background.